ANIMAL SUPERSTARS

BEAVER

MASTER BUILDER

PAIGE V. POLINSKY

CONSULTING EDITOR, DIANE CRAIG, M.A./READING SPECIALIST

Super Sandcastle

An Imprint of Abdo Publishing
abdopublishing.com

abdopublishing.com

Published by Abdo Publishing, a division of ABDO, PO Box 398166, Minneapolis, Minnesota 55439. Copyright © 2017 by Abdo Consulting Group, Inc. International copyrights reserved in all countries. No part of this book may be reproduced in any form without written permission from the publisher. Super SandCastle™ is a trademark and logo of Abdo Publishing.

Printed in the United States of America, North Mankato, Minnesota
062016
092016

Editor: Rebecca Felix
Content Developer: Nancy Tuminelly
Cover and Interior Design and Production: Christa Schneider, Mighty Media, Inc.
Photo Credits: iStockphoto; Mighty Media, Inc.; Shutterstock

Library of Congress Cataloging-in-Publication Data

Names: Polinsky, Paige V., author.
Title: Beaver : master builder / by Paige V. Polinsky.
Description: Minneapolis, Minnesota : Abdo Publishing, [2017] I Series:
  Animal superstars
Identifiers: LCCN 2016006305 (print) I LCCN 2016007036 (ebook) I ISBN
  9781680781465 (print) I ISBN 9781680775891 (ebook)
Subjects: LCSH: Beavers--Juvenile literature.
Classification: LCC QL737.R632 P65 2016 (print) I LCC QL737.R632 (ebook) I
  DDC 599.37--dc23
LC record available at http://lccn.loc.gov/2016006305

Super SandCastle™ books are created by a team of professional educators, reading specialists, and content developers around five essential components—phonemic awareness, phonics, vocabulary, text comprehension, and fluency—to assist young readers as they develop reading skills and strategies and increase their general knowledge. All books are written, reviewed, and leveled for guided reading, early reading intervention, and Accelerated Reader™ programs for use in shared, guided, and independent reading and writing activities to support a balanced approach to literacy instruction.

CONTENTS

REMARKABLE RODENTS

Beavers are large **rodents**. They are the second-largest rodents in the world! Adult beavers are about three feet (1 m) long. They weigh up to 60 pounds (27 kg).

CONSTRUCTION KINGS

North American beavers live in forests. Some were brought to South America. Eurasian beavers live in European and Asian forests.

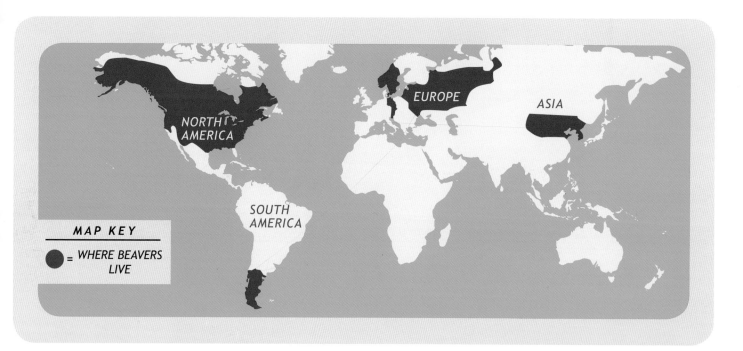

NORTH
AMERICA

EUROPE

ASIA

SOUTH
AMERICA

MAP KEY

● = WHERE BEAVERS
LIVE

HOW LONG?

Beavers chop down trees and build dams. One beaver dam can flood a field! This creates a safe **site** for beavers to build a home.

LOVELY LODGES

Beaver homes are called lodges. They are built on water. They are made of branches and mud. Most lodges have two underwater entrances. They also have eating areas and main living areas.

BEAVER BUILT

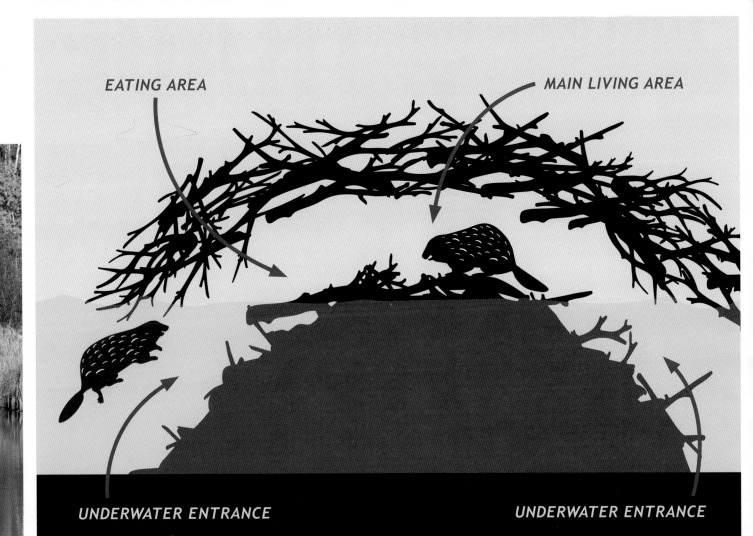

EATING AREA

MAIN LIVING AREA

UNDERWATER ENTRANCE

UNDERWATER ENTRANCE

TOOLS OF THE TRADE

Beavers are born to build. Their **chisel**-shaped teeth are coated in iron. This is a strong, hard metal. It makes the teeth extra strong. Beavers' wide, flat tails help them balance. This is helpful while carrying logs.

LOTS OF CHEWING

BEAVER TEETH NEVER STOP GROWING. CHEWING WOOD WEARS THEM DOWN. THIS KEEPS THEM FROM GETTING TOO LONG.

BUSY BUILDERS

Beavers work together to gather wood. First, one beaver chews through a tree trunk. Its mate then helps chew the trunk into logs. Together, they float the logs to their dam or lodge.

A beaver can chew through a 6-inch (l5 cm) trunk in less than 30 minutes!

CLEVER COLLECTING

Beavers eat twigs, leaves, and water plants. In autumn, beavers gather a lot of food. They store it underwater. This becomes their winter **pantry**!

WATER WONDERS

Beavers are great swimmers. Their **webbed** back feet act as flippers. Their tails help them steer. Their fur is thick and oily. It is **waterproof.**

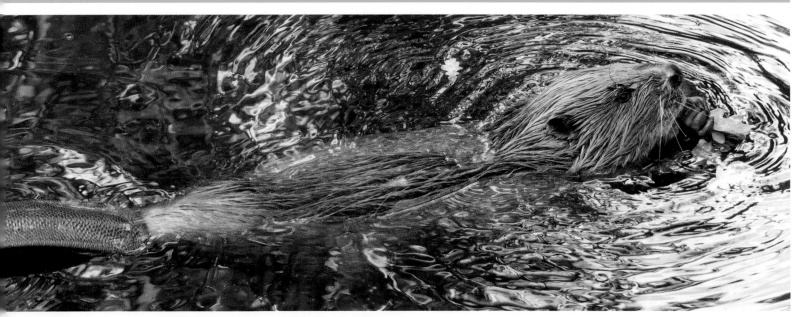

FOREVER FAMILIES

Beavers mate for life. Females birth one to nine **kits** each year.

HANDY HELPERS

Young beavers live in the family lodge for about two years.
They help watch over younger **kits**.

A YOUNG BEAVER

BEAVER KITS

CLOSE CALL

Humans used to trap beavers for their fur. They used it to make clothing. By the 1900s, beavers were almost **extinct**. Luckily, beaver fur became unpopular. Today there are many of these large **rodents**.

WATER WARNING!

BEAVERS WARN EACH OTHER OF DANGER. TO DO THIS, THEY SLAP THEIR TAILS AGAINST THE WATER.

BEAVER SUPERSTAR

Can you imagine a beaver superstar? What **awards** would it win?

WHAT DO YOU KNOW ABOUT
BEAVERS?

1. Beavers are the world's second-largest **rodent**.

True or false?

3. Beavers mainly eat fish and small turtles.

True or false?

2. Beaver homes are called lodges.

True or false?

4. Beavers mate for life.

True or false?

ANSWERS:
1. TRUE 2. TRUE 3. FALSE 4. TRUE

GLOSSARY

AWARD - a prize.

CHISEL - a tool with a flat, sharp end that is used to cut and shape a solid material such as stone, wood, or metal.

EXTINCT - no longer existing.

KIT - a young fur-bearing animal.

PANTRY - a room or closet used for food storage.

RODENT - a mammal with large, sharp front teeth, such as a beaver, mouse, or squirrel.

SITE - location.

WATERPROOF - made to keep water out.

WEBBED - having toes connected by a web or fold of skin.